Bed Hangings

by Susan Howe

pictures by Susan Bee

To other lands Liberticide
Lucifer has winged his wayward past

BED HANGINGS

by Susan Howe

pictures by Susan Bee

Granary Books · New York · 2001

Copyright © 2001 Susan Howe, Susan Bee and Granary Books

All rights reserved. No parts of this book may be reproduced
without express written permission of the authors.

Printed and bound in the United States of America
Printed on acid-free paper

Library of Congress Cataloging-in-Publication Data
is available for this title

Granary Books, Inc.
307 Seventh Ave. Suite 1401
New York, NY 10001
www.granarybooks.com

Distributed to the trade by
D.A.P/Distributed Art Publishers
155 Avenue of the Americas, Second Floor
New York, NY 10013-1507
Orders: (800) 338-BOOK
Tel. (212) 627-1999 • Fax (212) 627-9484

For here we are here

BED HANGINGS

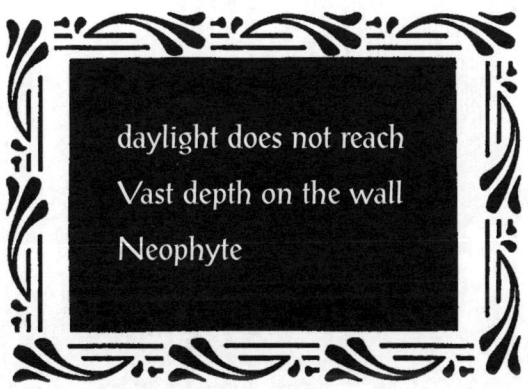

daylight does not reach
Vast depth on the wall
Neophyte

Alapeen Paper Patch Muslin
Calico Camlet Dimity Fustian
Serge linsey-woolsey say

A wainscot bedsted & Curtans
& vallains & iron Rodds
Many bedsteds were roped
"Bedsted. . . . & bed Rope

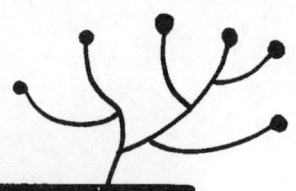

Revisionist work in
historic interiors spread
from House to Museum

Other documentary evidence
Friends who wish to
remain anonymous

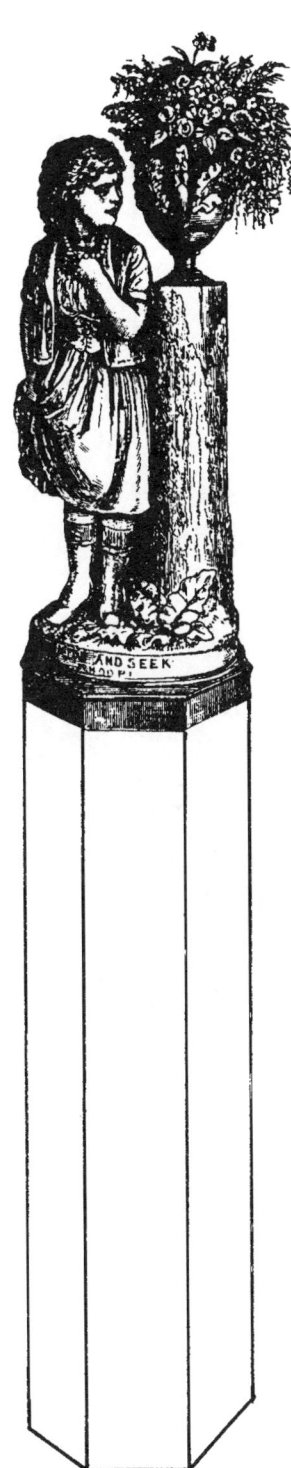

Contest between two
singers *Conflictus ovis
et lini* if the heart or
eye were cause of sin
Rival claims Summer
Winter Soul Body Wine
Water Phillis Flora

Ordered wigs cloaks
breeches hoods gowns
rings jewels necklaces
to be brought together

One of the perplexing questions on which members of the Bed Curtain Seminar were able to shed very little light was that of how early valences attached to the tester frame **Technical Note** Other rubbish a bottomless chair

Go to my savage pattern
on surface material the line
in ink if you have curtains
and a New English dictionary
there is nothing to justify a
claim for linen except a late
quotation knap warp is flax
Fathom we without cannot

Research projects the 1960
seminar on bedhangings

Scholar student participant
Published papers remain
Say flowing forces haunt
leaving no shade pattern
Why huntress why pattern

A small swatch bluish-green
woolen slight grain in the
weft watered and figured
right fustian should hold
altogether warp and woof
Is the cloven rock misled
Does morning lie what prize
What pine tree wildeyed boy

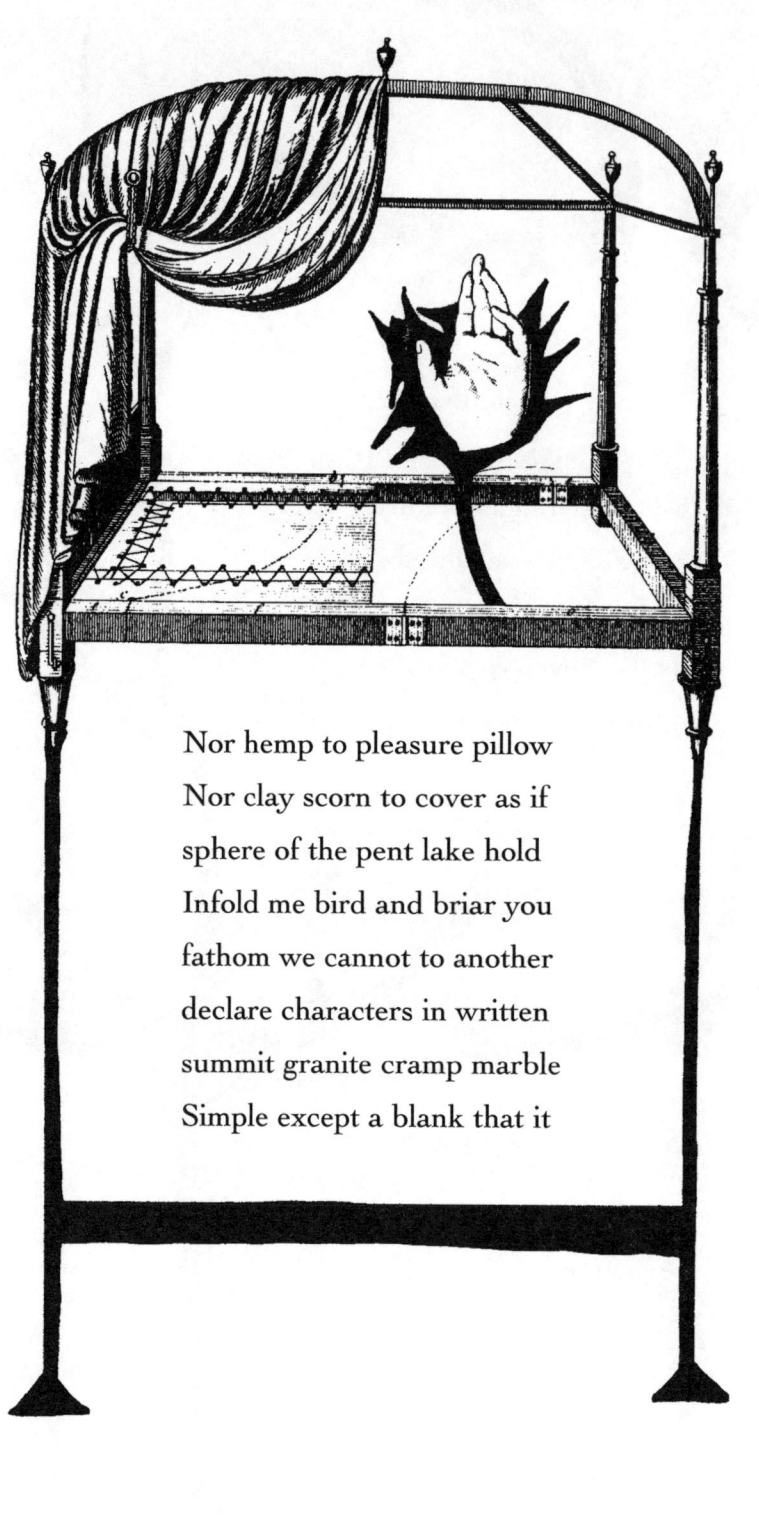

Nor hemp to pleasure pillow
Nor clay scorn to cover as if
sphere of the pent lake hold
Infold me bird and briar you
fathom we cannot to another
declare characters in written
summit granite cramp marble
Simple except a blank that it

Present present *presentness*
High mahogany bed roods &
rails do ring loop ties back
A sets down and C takes up
conformity to that uniformity
Ownership and ownership it
is a maxim of logic the Double
of the object is that I desire it

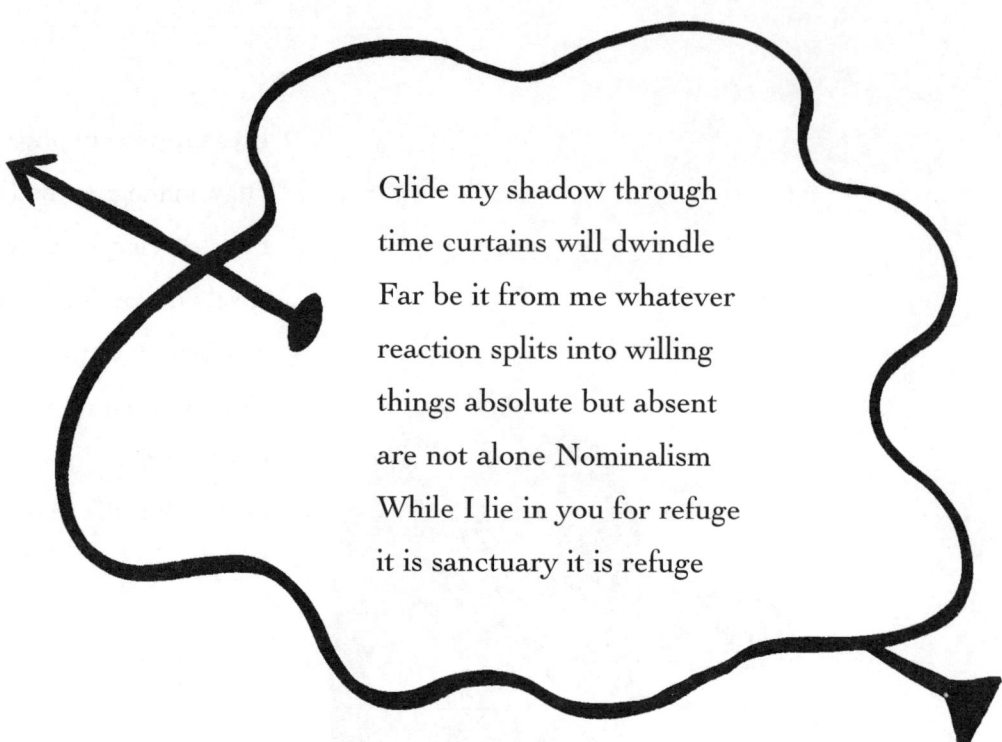

Glide my shadow through
time curtains will dwindle
Far be it from me whatever
reaction splits into willing
things absolute but absent
are not alone Nominalism
While I lie in you for refuge
it is sanctuary it is refuge

Three friends who wish to
remain anonymous a first
design how it was nursed
for cimmerian subtlety for
versification a counterpane
has no reason being agent
Whilst for an absent friend–
Low adamantine net fringe

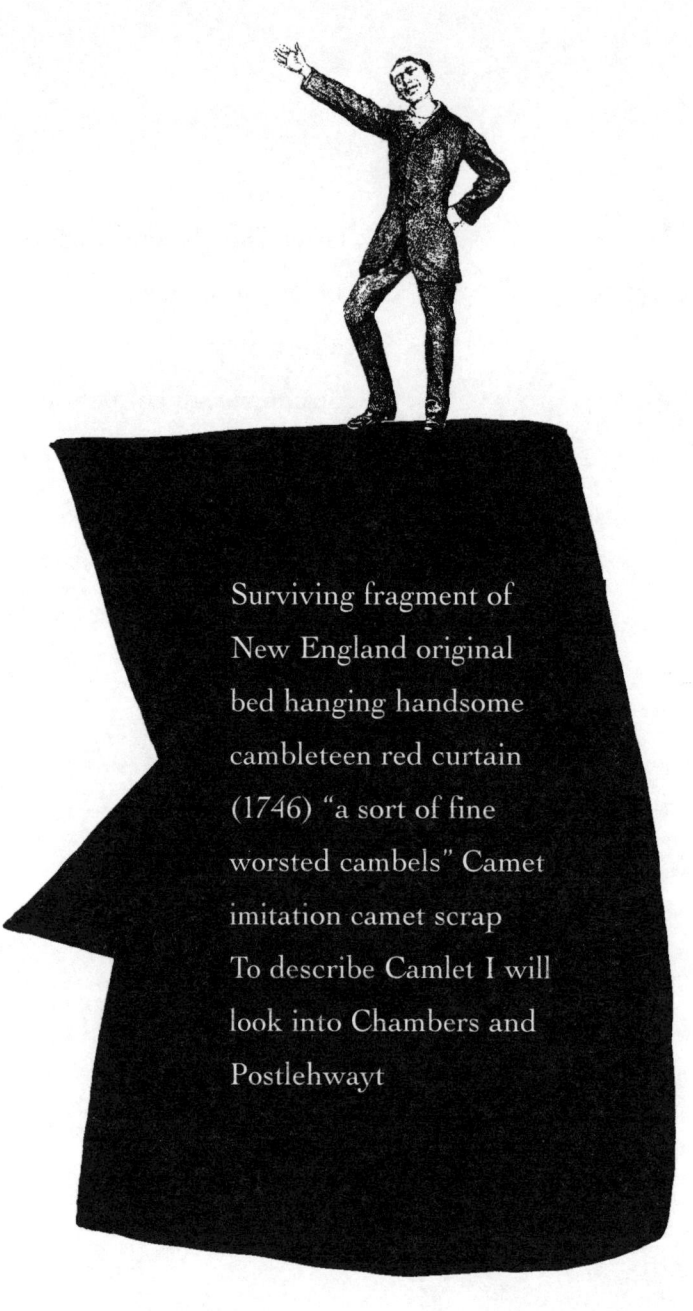

Surviving fragment of
New England original
bed hanging handsome
cambleteen red curtain
(1746) "a sort of fine
worsted cambels" Camet
imitation camet scrap
To describe Camlet I will
look into Chambers and
Postlehwayt

1746 (fig 39) A figured head cloth worked by Polly Wright of Hatfield Massachusetts in 1765 (privately owned) This curtain fabric of "moreen" by a donor born in 1836 A swatch and swatches described as "harateen" Owner John Holker 1850

Counterforce bring me wild hope
non-connection is itself distinct
connection numerous surviving
fair trees wrought with a needle
the merest decorative suggestion
in what appears to be sheer white
muslin a tree fair hunted Daphne
Thinking is willing you are wild
to the weave not to material itself

Upon the interpreter this ambush
Theory at war with phenomena
Thought or form handsbreadth
though paper tossed overboard
can have been conversely tossed
back to background as if woof
warp theory the real what is real
Night draws the planet tremulous
Tinsel hope I intersect linen silk

The ego securely undaunted elect
as pedigree might seem to sound
Example reveals pierced interval
eyelet holes though admittedly if
emblem tossed it lends progress
a corporeal incorporeal European
argument of intellectual sympathy
Sphere of the pent lake hold flint
The ambush lay in wanton purpose

Soon swerved from what
people of his charge took him
to be

Not only alone but on foot
with his luggage on his back
On the first of January 1801

Something over against is
what surprised the sadder
and wiser

Sandemanian sentiments of course he never preached as the denomination admits no correlative save Christ and his apostles for the rote of ethic Embracing the sentiments of the Sandemanians he was dismissed and his apostle until the church became extinct a study of odd relic aforesaid

You disconcert a maxim
of Pragmatism scorning
small doses of induction
Pragmaticism so far as it
goes if A is true C is true
What is it that is absolute
This is not shown at all
Proceeding to the wood
along with some coeval
you hope to fell a first tree

You are he who felled by tree deducts the maxims of Pragmatism scorning by a point propitious abduction hedged by paper you appear to me walking across the text to call an unconverted soul King James lyricism another C minor Coeval decades hereafter

Ten thousandth truth
Ten thousandth impulse
Do not mince matter
as if tumbling were apt
parable preached in
hedge-sparrow gospel
For the lily welcomes
Owl! art thou mad?
Why dost thou twit me
with foreknowledge

To this the Nihtegale gave answer that twig of thine thou shouldst sing another tune Owl Still in Ovid cloth of scarlet the Owl and her "Old Side" blue thread Listen! Let me speak! the Wren replied I do not want lawlessness

Everyone knows in a rough way
the impious history of sensation
Earlier times resemble ice to the
fourth parish or enthusiast class
Sheets and pillows are initiated
Permanent thought permanent
Before inviolate love knots are
edged with paper in the manner
of braided binding valences before
a long night's sleep with closure

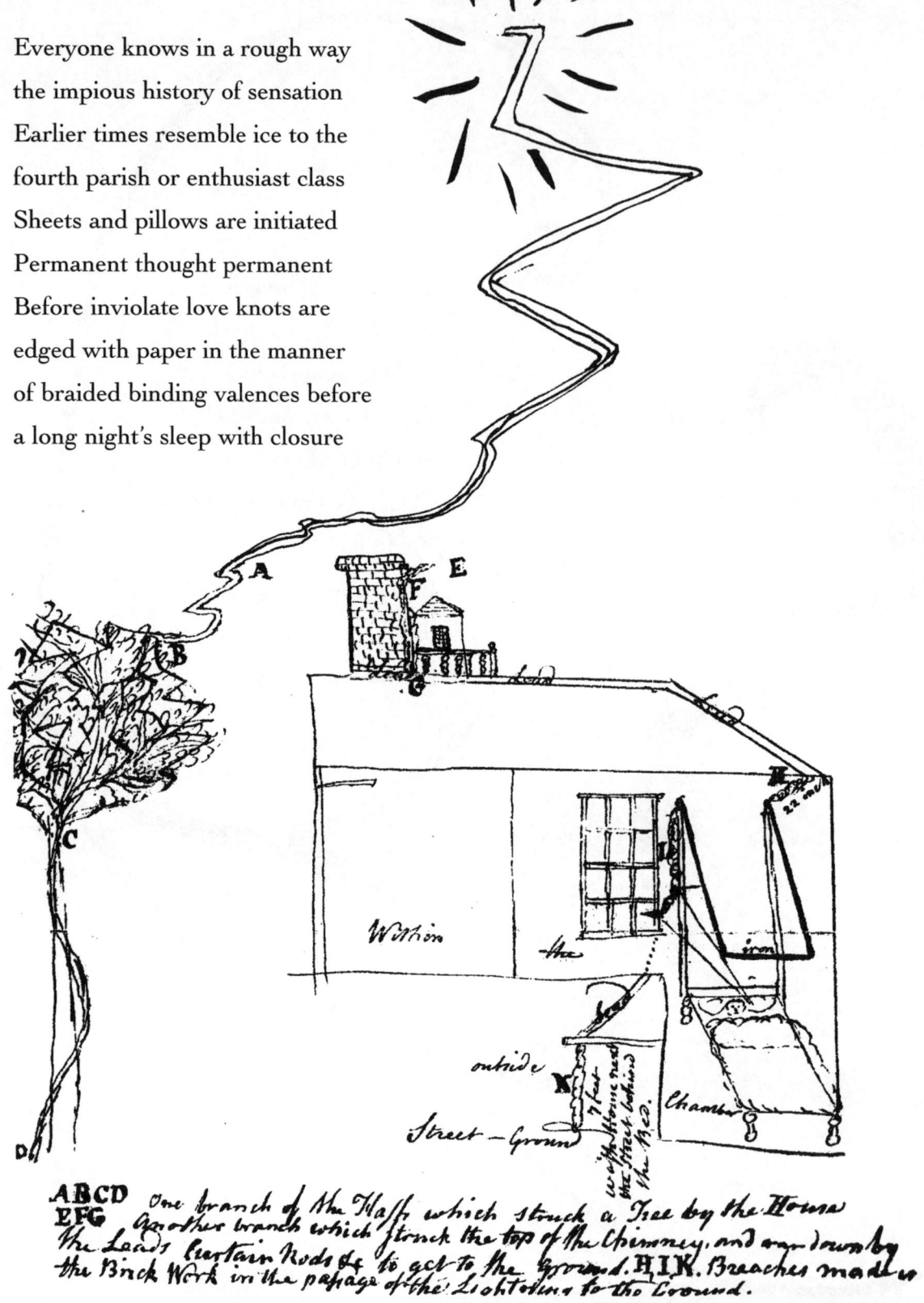

Evening for the Owl
spoke wisely and well
willing to suffer them
and come flying night
from the Carolingian
mid owl falcon fable
In their company saw
all things clearly wel
Unfele I could not do

Nihtegale to the taunt
Owl a preost be piping
Overgo al spoke iseon
sede warme inome nv
stille one bare worde
Go he started mid ivi
Grene al never ne nede
Song long ago al so
sumere chorless awey

Milk they drink and also whey they
know not otherwise bitter accent
I do not remember any crying out
falling down or fainting to signify
revelation preached from Isaiah 60
I have not known visions trances
Who are they that fly as a cloud as
doves to their windows have pity
From terrible and deep conviction
Brandish unreconciled yet arrows

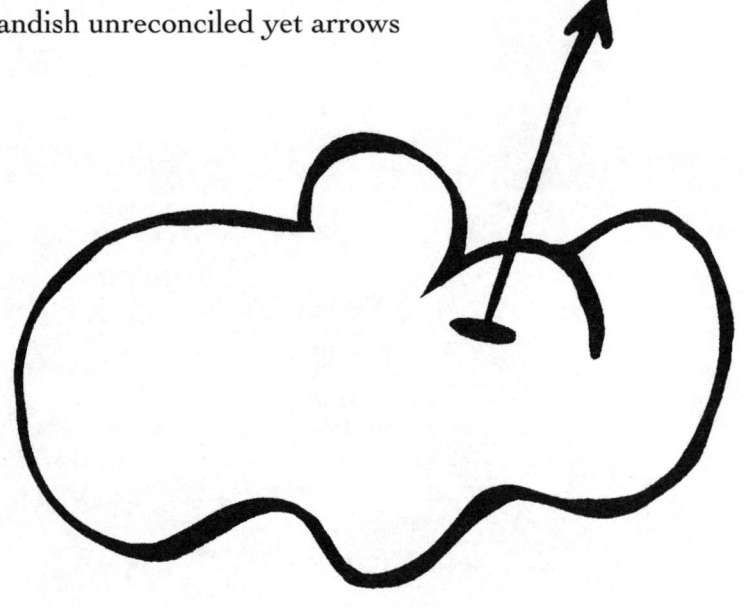

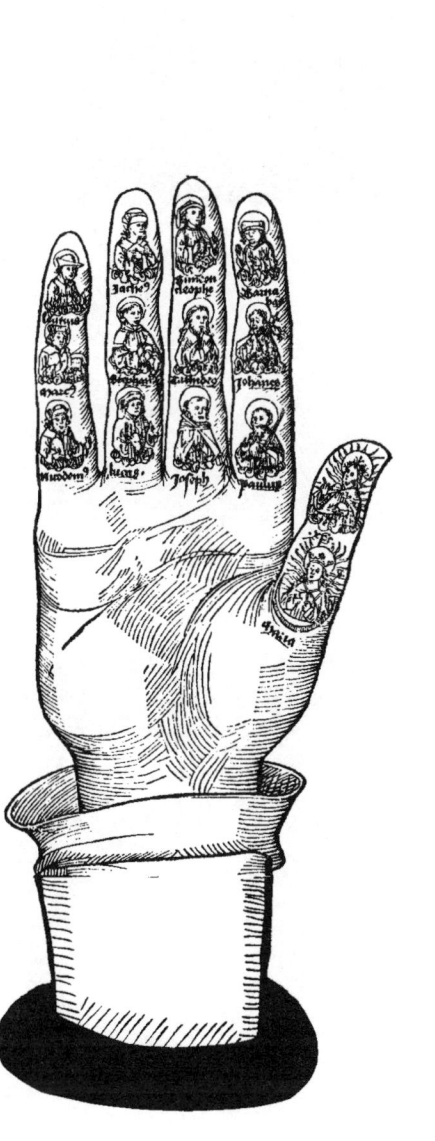

Pensive itinerants and exhorters gathering manna in the morning Thirty pages then the rest mostly children enact ruin enthusiastical impressions in my mind though not to my knowledge it seems he still believed he was conversing with an invisible spirit however the sharp weather his wet jacket Finding himself alive went home

On Our Most Beautiful and Precious Beaker

In 1668 another beaker thought necessary for the large Meeting House built in 1713 was the gift of Madame Ruth Naughty who had given her black slave Moses to Mr. Fowler she bequeathed £4 to purchase the beaker which bears her name

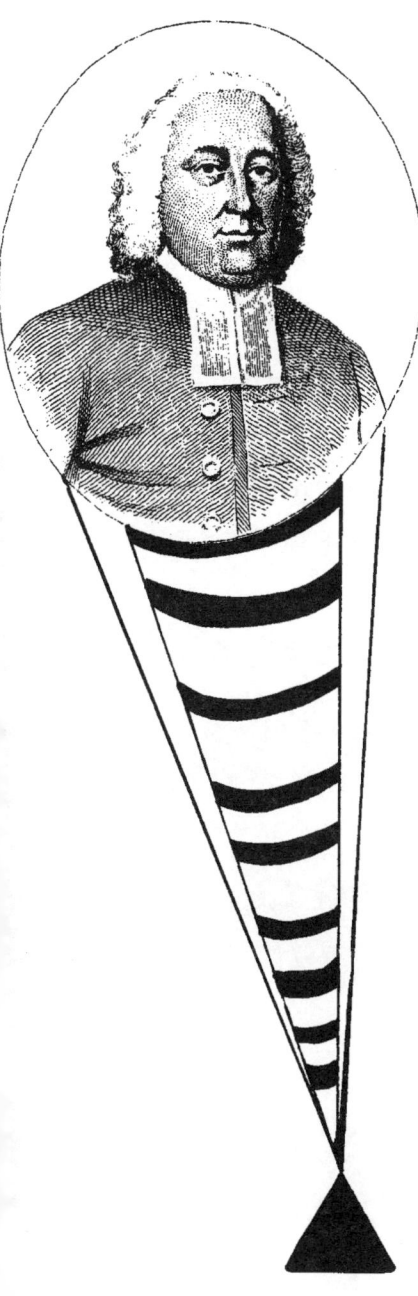

Something over against Mr. Sprout

He can be found in the cool of evening rolling in his chaise with his shepherdess Wearing a large Presbyterian cloak somewhat soiled with a full bestowed wig a month or six weeks diligence will teach him the exercise of the windpipe

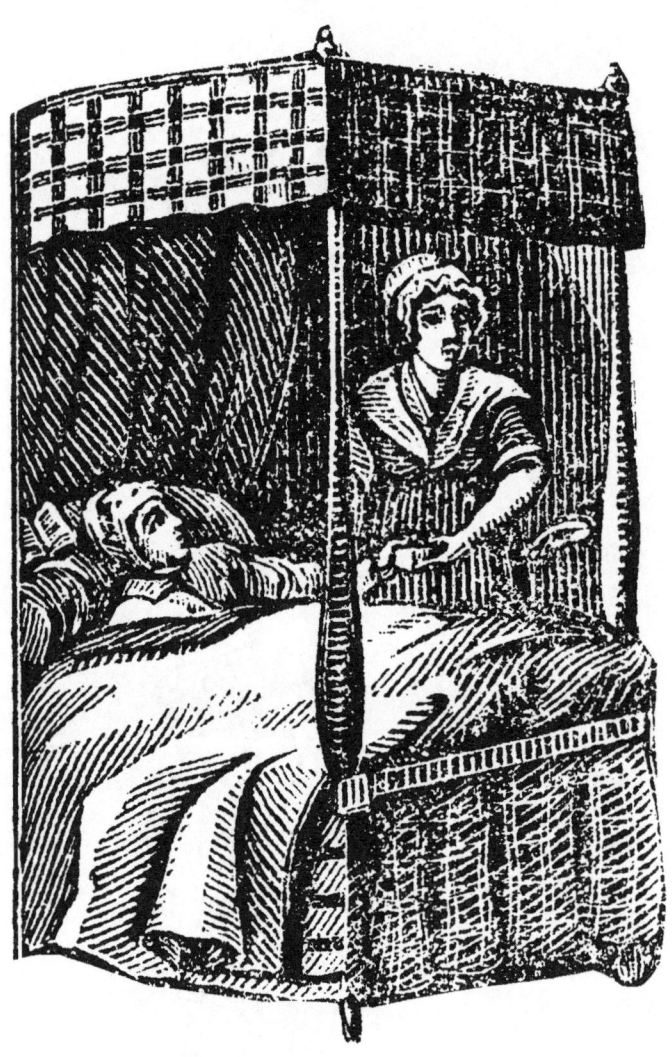

Some prepared cloth or other
left simply in the hair 'glazed'
or 'lustred' a kind of twilled
lasting when stouter John Legg
of Boston left to his daughter
1 Coach bed camblet curtanot
vallens to disenchant blessing
All lands and to the bordering

Malachy Postlehwayt (ed.1773)
defines Calamanco as "a woolen
stuff manufactured in Brabant
in Flanders" checquered in warp
wherein the warp is mixed with
silk or with goat's hair diversely
wrought yet some are quite plain
When did appearance ever justify

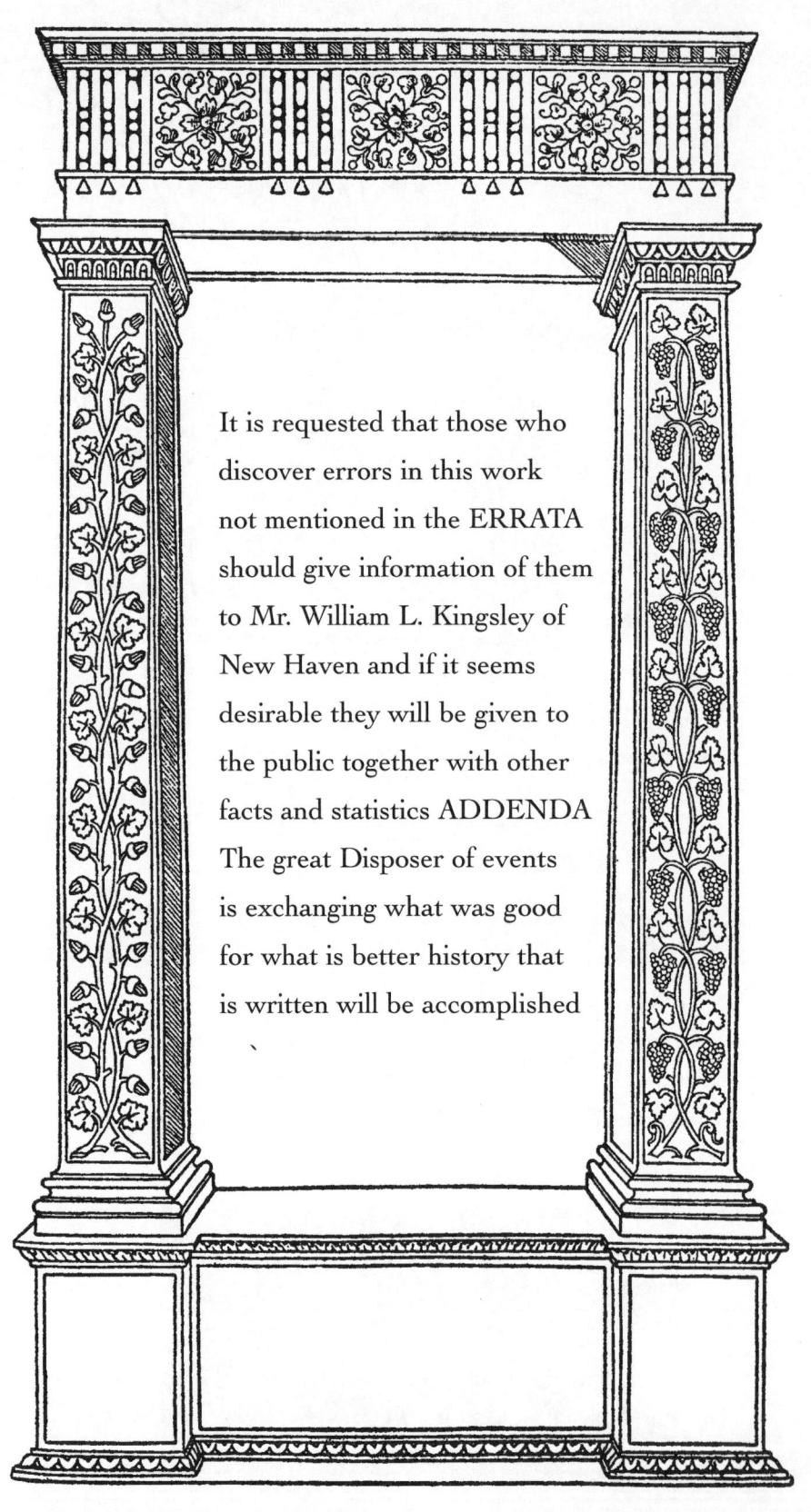

Stille one bare worde
iseon at bare beode
iseon at bare beode

Fleao westerness iseo
Opertuo go andsware

EPILOGUE

Bed, n. a couch to sleep on; a bank of earth; channel of a river; a layer; stratum.
Cur'tain, n. (kur'tin) a cloth hanging round a bed, at a window, or in a theatre.
Hang'ing, n. drapery hung to the walls of rooms.
Hang'man, n. a public executioner.
Test'er, n. a sixpence, the cover of a bed.

    J.E. Wooster, *An Elementary Dictionary for Common Schools*, Boston and Philadelphia, 1839.

"'Causing his servant to leave him unusually one morning, locking himselfe in, he strangled himselfe with his cravatt upon the bed-tester. —Evelyn, Diary, Aug. 18, 1673.'"

    cited in W. D. Whitney, *The Century Dictionary and Cyclopedia*, New York, 1889.

❀   ❀   ❀   ❀

    I am an insomniac who goes to bed in a closet.
    "AWAKE, *a*, not sleeping; in a state of vigilance or action." "AWAKENING, *n*. A revival of religion, or more general attention to religion than usual." Although these are Noah Webster's definitions, out of his writing speaks Calvin. For Calvin the Bible contains two kinds of knowledge—ecstatic union and law. In *An American Dictionary of the English Language* a curtain is a cloth hanging used in theaters to conceal the stage from the spectators, while an itinerant is someone who travels from place to place and is unsettled; particularly a preacher. One Sunday afternoon in the gift shop at Hartford's Wadsworth Athenaeum, wandering among the postcards, notepaper, ties, scarves, necklaces, keychains, calendars, magic markers, pens, pencils, posters, children's games, paperweights, and art books, displayed to be worshipped or

acquired, my attention came to rest on a pedestrian gray paperback. I was preparing to teach a graduate seminar on what has been called "The Great Awakening" of the 1740s. This intercolonial religious revival, with its growth of an itinerant ministry and field sermons, swept through the Connecticut River Valley, then considered back country, in the wake of the arrival of the English evangelist preacher George Whitefield in 1739 (David Garrick said Whitefield could make his hearers weep or tremble at pleasure, by his varied utterance of the word 'Mesopotamia') and Jonathan Edwards' restrained but furious eloquence ("Sinners in the Hands of an Angry God; A Sermon Preached at Enfield, July 8th 1741, At a Time of Great Awakenings; and attended with remarkable Impressions on many of the Hearers"). When Europe enters the space of its margin, the "Kingdom of God in America" receives European memory into itself. In thin places bedsteads confront their own edges. English actors and English ministers play key roles in eighteenth century Revivalism. Sometimes charismatic itinerant ministers have no doctrinal or institutional affiliations. Field beds have canopies at the top resembling tents. *Bed Hangings: A Treatise on Fabrics and Styles in the Curtaining of Beds, 1650-1850* with its drab cover illustration, a detail of the East Chamber, Peter Cushing House, Hingham, Mass., painted by Ella Emory in 1878 for the Society for the Preservation of New England Antiquities, struck me as vividly apropos. I wondered who tipped over the vase of flowers to the left of the bed in the painted East Chamber? Did the spilled flowers suggest a stray sense of comedy or inspired simplicity?

❊ ❊ ❊

Seven of Emerson's ancestors were ministers in New England churches. In his twenties he hoped he might "put on eloquence like a robe," and he left the ministry to become a lecturer/performer. Years later when reading aloud Aytoun's lines in "The Burial March of Dundee—" "What parts, what gems, what colors shine,—/ Ah, but I miss the grand design," he is said to have paused and added, "The upholsterer!"

❋ ❋ ❋

"*Nominalism. n.* The doctrine that nothing is general but names; more specifically the doctrine that common nouns, as man, horse, represent in their generality nothing in the real things, but are mere conveniences for speaking of many things at once, or at most necessities of human thought; individualism." Charles Sanders Peirce wrote this definition of nominalism, a doctrine he abhorred, for William Dwight Whitney's *Century Dictionary* (1889). One of his earliest memories was of being taken to hear Emerson lecture. Another early memory was playing rapid games of double dummy from ten in the evening until sunrise with his father, the mathematician Benjamin Peirce. In Dummy at *Whist*, an imaginary player represented by an exposed 'hand' is managed by and serves as partner to one of the players. In Double Dummy two 'hands' are exposed so each of the players manages two exposed 'hands' at once. Naturally Peirce became an insomniac.

❋ ❋ ❋

Often, during the early morning hours between 3am and 7am, when I should be unconscious in my closet, I remain horribly conscious. Especially around Halloween when time is forced to fall back so daybreak comes even earlier. Then I wonder bitterly why we ever did away with bed presses like the one (built into the wall) in the Stephen Wing House, in East Sandwich, Mass., ca. 1750-55, and I remember my eccentric great aunt Mabel Quincy Davis who lived at the decaying Lenox Hotel in Boston during the 1950s. On those nights when the hour fell back, or sprang forward, she repeatedly phoned the front desk to ask "How are we getting on?"

A source for this book is *Bed Hangings:*
A Treatise on Fabrics and Styles in the Curtaining of Beds, 1650-1850
compiled by Abbott Lowell Cummings
Boston, Mass.: Society for thePreservation
of New England Antiquities, 1994.

Printed and bound at McNaughton & Gunn
in an edition of one thousand copies
of which twenty-six are lettered
and signed by poet and artist.